THE ART OF SELLING YOUR ART

Danilo Di Nuzzo

The Art of Selling Your Art
By Danilo Di Nuzzo
2020

TO WORK WITH DANILO PLEASE E-MAIL TO:
danilo8@iol.it
IG: @el_arte_de_vender_tu_arte

Translation in English by Rebecca Melara
Designed by Alexander Mendoza

ÍNDICE

C'e' una persona che riesce a motivarmi, ogni volta che ne ho bisogno. Ci riesce sempre, anche a diecimila chilometri di distanza. E' riuscita ad incoraggiarmi a scrivere questo libro anche senza sapere che lo stessi scrivendo. Dedico questo lavoro alla piu' bella opera d'arte che io abbia mai potuto ammirare:

MIA MADRE.

There is a person that motivates whenever I need it. She always accomplishes it, even if she's ten thousand kilometers away. She has pushed me to write this book without knowing that I had already started writing it. I dedicate this work to the most beautiful work of art that I have ever laid eyes upon.

MY MOTHER.

INTRODUCTION

If you are an artist and have decided that you want to make a living by selling your art, it's better that you have a clear basic concept on how you would like to construct your professional career. Making a living off of your art consists in creating pieces and selling them to clients. The same as for any business that earns revenue by selling their manufactured products. If you are an artist, you will surely be more prepared on topics related to the art world rather than with commercial sales strategies. To simplify the proper assimilation of this concept and the execution of an action plan I will divide your work into two categories: PRODUCTION and SALES.

For the suitable production of your pieces, there are several subcategories of things you have to work on as an artist such as: artistic technique, material, inspiration, motivation, optimization and anything that is related to your work process. On this topic, I cannot help you because I'm neither an art professor nor am I qualified on any subject related to artistic production. If you need any help in this field, there are several experts that can help you on being more creative, productive and innovative in your creation process. In this book, you will find a summarized action plan for the correct commercialization and SALE of your art pieces. Some paragraphs contain concepts that are the basis of any commercial strategy and that work for any type of sale regardless of what the final product is.

Other paragraphs talk about very specific strategies that only work in the commercialization of art pieces. What you need to understand is that there is no successful artist that has overlooked any of these two categories. Success is not achieved by luck. Success is the result of a series of strategies and actions executed with discipline and consistency. Concentrate on adequately planning the production of your art pieces and work to improve your sales strategies and you will see how your art pieces will find buyers, as a logical consequence of a properly executed plan.

Remember, that the harvest comes only after having plowed, sowed and taken proper care of your field. If you skip any of these steps, you will not be able to reap what you have sowed. If you are an artist and want to make a living doing what you love, you have to do the same things as any successful company: create products that are true to the brand and sell it at the best price. If your commercial strategies are bad, your sales will be bad and this will unleash economic problems, stress, depression and lack of enthusiasm. This will all affect your motivation and inspiration to produce more pieces and as a result you will have very few and/or lower quality pieces to sell. It's like a cat the bites its own tail. In the end you could abandon your dream of being an artist while ending up in a job you don't like just to make ends meet. If you learn to sell your art pieces, you could make a living and earn money doing what you really love: BEING AN ARTIST.

You can live an economically stable life by selling your art. Learn how to do it and apply it to your life. You can start one minute after you have finished this book.

Keep your head up and enjoy reading this book!

CHAPTER 1

CURRENT SITUATION

1.1 Why are my pieces not selling as well as I would like them to?

If you are finding it difficult to find buyers for your pieces, it means that you are not selling them properly. You can even consider lowering the asking price and you will realize that it will not make that much of a difference.

Why? The answer is you are lacking a proper customized action plan and commercial strategy for your type of art. Any artist who is now successful, first constructed their own signature style that can be seen in all their pieces, permitting them to stand out from the crowd. Thanks to this personal style, audiences can easily identify and appreciate a work of art without even reading the signature. If you can accomplish this, it means that you will have established a solid reputation in which to build your professional career around. Once you have done this, you can proceed to working the commercial aspect and build YOUR COMPANY AS AN ARTIST.

If you want to make a living off of selling your art, you have to pay close attention to the commercial aspect of your profession. Sales will not come on their own. Works of art are not only sold because of their beauty and aesthetic, they always need someone with the ability to sell them.

This someone has to be you. If you are not willing to take care of this aspect of your business, then you will probably not reach a level in which you can quit your day job and live solely out of the income generated by selling your art pieces. In business, no one can afford to create and manufacture excellent products without selling it to anybody.

To create a masterpiece, you have to be inspired and artistically prepared. To sell it, you must be motivated and be knowledgeable in sales strategies. Do not worry if you believe you are not a good salesperson. Sales techniques can be learned easily, you just have to be aware of the fact that you need to dedicate time into learning and applying them.

Good quality art pieces that are put up for sale always find buyers willing to pay whatever the asking price is. You will have to plan sales and marketing strategies ahead. Later on, you will have to execute them. Every successful artist in their professional career has something in common: THEY FOLLOW A PLAN. Keep your head up and good luck with yours!

1.2 What is this book and what is it for?

I wrote this book because of my wish to help artists to sell their works of art. Despite the importance of sales in the art world, nobody teaches this subject in art academies. The lack of preparation in this subject matter is a problem that affects every student who is finishing their academic journey and are about to enter the working world. Many students who finish college and university studies and want to work as independent professionals, first need to be interns for a specific amount of time and pass an exam that permits them to execute a specific profession. Guess what? Nobody ever teaches students throughout their entire academic career HOW TO SELL THEIR PRODUCTS OR SERVICES.

For example, an independent lawyer has to practice his profession by selling his services to private clients. His or her success and economic stability will not only depend on his/her qualifications for practicing law, it will also depend on his/her ability to sell themselves as a professional. The same goes with any other profession. In any academic program, they teach you how to execute any specific profession but rarely how to monetize them. It's a fundamental subject that is preventing most students from becoming a complete professional. Knowing how to sell permits young professionals to monetize the knowledge they acquired in school. If you are an artist and you wish to MAKE A LIVING off your art, you have to learn how to sell your pieces. Generally speaking, most artists lack basic knowledge of sales strategies. There are very talented artists that have to quit their dream because they aren't capable of selling their pieces. In most cases, they don't sell because they don't know how to do it. They do one or several things wrong and at the end are not able to pay their living expenses and live an economically stable life. It is possible to monetize your pieces if you follow a proper marketing and sales plan. This applies to all types of products. Even companies such as Ferrari, Coca-Cola and Apple, need to develop a carefully designed action plan in order to sell. The purpose of this book is not to entertain you as a romance novel would do. It represents a tool whose final goal is to teach you how to EARN MONEY AND MAKE A LIVING OFF OF YOUR ART.

This is why I have tried to be clear and concise while summarizing the entire lesson and tips as much as possible. I have chosen only the basic and specific topics you need to cover to help you accomplish your dream. I want to take you from point A to point B using the shortest way possible without any unnecessary detour.

1.3 I am an artist and want to earn money

Up to a few years ago, being a full-time artist was a synonym of financial struggle. This does not necessarily mean that all artists in the past have been poor, but it was the case for most of them, even for the artists who were very accomplished.

We have always been influenced on how we perceive artists. Most people associate artists with people who suffer substance abuse or live a very modest life associated to a bohemian style. In fact, there are many examples of famous artists that did just that including Modigliani, Van Gogh, Gauguin. They all lived a very modest life despite their artistic genius. This profession was almost always a synonym of living modestly except of course for those artists involved in creating commissioned art for churches, royal and noble families, etc. Most other artists lived in extreme poverty conditions.

Sometimes, they couldn't even contact the only people that had the economic position to purchase their art. This has changed throughout the years especially due to the Internet. Being an artist now a days has enormous advantages over the artists of the past. Imagine what could have been for Vincent Van Gogh if he had had the possibility of placing his art in social media platforms such as Instagram and the opportunity to sell his masterpieces online.

We can never know for sure but we do know that his artistic genius combined with the potential these current tools offer, the results would have been magnificent. If you are a talented artist, you have to use all the available tools that exist now a days. If you want to LIVE OFF OF YOUR ART, there is no better and easier time than today.

1.4 Why are there so many struggling artists in the world?

The answer is very simple: they do not use the tools they have at their disposal. In many cases, they completely ignore them and that's why I decided to write this book.

An artist is generally a person that wants to dedicate their time and creativity to create pieces of art, leaving all other important aspects aside such as public relations, marketing strategies, sales strategies and many more subjects that we will dive into in the next chapters. Following the step by step instructions explained in this book, you will be able to maximize the sales potential of your work and build a profitable career as an artist. You will be able to sell many pieces in very little time at the best price.

If you are barely starting your career as an artist, you are probably not earning enough money from selling your pieces. You may at times feel depressed and lacking motivation. You are probably thinking that it would be best to leave your passion aside and start looking for a "normal" job. Don't do it. You have to learn how to EARN MONEY SELLING YOUR ART PIECES.

You can start with a very low investment, there are low-cost and effective ways to showcase your pieces to the entire world. I will not talk about how to produce your own works of art nor will I talk about what is trending these days in the art world. This is something every artist should cover with experts on the subject. We are not going to talk about how to find inspiration when creating your art and how to improve certain techniques. I love art, but I am not an expert on the creation process. If you have artistic talent and your pieces are of good quality, technically speaking, and audiences generally like them, this will depend on you and you only. If you need advice on how to create a masterpiece, I recommend you seek an expert on this topic. I cannot assure you that your art pieces will be successful in today's competitive market, but I can guarantee that there is a process that is going to permit you to showcase you're your works of art to the entire world and eventually convert this interest into sales. This is a plan to create a brand as an artist, to properly market it and sell your work. It's quite easy to execute as long as you follow the steps with consistency and determination.

1.5 Are you already a successful artist?

If you are already famous and are already earning a sufficient amount of money by selling your art, surely you have done something right. This is quite obvious because you have clearly obtained positive results. For you, reading THE ART OF SELLING ART means that you simply want to confirm the things that you have done that have helped you succeed. But you are also probably wondering if there are ways to increase your currents sales?

Unless your name is Fernando Botero, there are many things that could help you optimize several aspects of YOUR COMPANY AS AN ARTIST. You can learn to minimize the expenses for the organization of events, further increase the visibility of your pieces and strongly invest more time in activities such as public relations and branding as an artist. This is about analyzing your profile and discovering what your strengths and weaknesses are. It is never too late to learn new things and improve your sales strategies in order to earn more money by selling your work.

1.6 Selling your pieces, differences between today and yesterday

The life of artists in the past years was generally hard. There was no internet, smartphones or computers. To showcase an art piece, they had to physically transport it to the potential buyer's location. Later on, with the invention of photography, they could photograph them. Those were the only ways were to reach any potential buyer. This is why artists as talented as Vincent Van Gogh had little success selling their work their entire lives. His art was unknown and misunderstood, therefore not awakening the buyer's interest. Now a days, an artist with Van Gogh's talent, that uses the Internet appropriately along with appropriate sales techniques, would sell many art pieces at high prices. He or she would be a very successful artist. There are still many very talented artists that struggle financially. This is mostly because they don't use the tools available to them to properly market their work.

The world's economy and ways to earn money has changed greatly. Also, artists have been affected by these changes and have to reinvent themselves in order to be successful. You have to learn to use these new sales tools in order to keep up with today's world. These tools will neither improve your artistic talent, nor the beauty of your work, but they can exponentially increase the way to show the world who you are as an artist, your different art pieces and the meaning behind each piece. This is what potential buyers love.

They want to see art pieces that they like and hear stories about them. They want to feel like there is a great person behind these works of art. Only then will they trust you as an artist and be willing to pay whatever price you choose for your work. Let's be clear: almost everyone that invests in art also pays attention to the price. Maybe many of them do not consider buying a piece expecting they can resell it for a profit later on. They do it because they like it and because they believe that the value of the piece will increase through time. That is why you have to create a good reputation as a professional artist, set a path and stay active and learn how to set the part. This way, buyers will be interested in you as an artist, in your path and your work. It is the only way you can sell your work at the best price.

1.7 Why do you have to be a good art salesperson?

If you are just starting a career as a professional artist, you are probably not earning enough money to make a living and you probably need to find other sources of income. Search for a job or project that can generate stable income with flexible hours that allow you to advance in your artistic career. You will be more occupied and tired, but you will surely be less stressed about personal financial issues. This way, you will have more peace of mind and inspiration to produce high quality art pieces. Every step you need to take to learn THE ART OF SELLING ART, can also be taken if you have a side job and cannot, for the moment, be a full-time artist. If you are determined and consistent you will eventually generate sales. It will not be through magic, it will be as a result of your actions.

Factors such as the price of a piece are not the most important or the only thing that can generate a sale. What will lead you to success in monetizing your art will be your financial education, your motivation and your ability to sell. To improve your financial education as well as your personal motivation, there are several books written by experts that have explained this topic in a very simple and summarized way. They teach you which are the best ways to think about money, which are the best ways to use it and how to always be motivated and determined.

I also recommend reading e-books or listening to audios on YouTube. It is an efficient and accessible way that you can use with the same frequency as a daily workout, for example. Motivation is like physical form, if you do not train enough, you could lose it.

To improve your sales pitch and maximize your economic benefits, you have to learn THE ART OF SELLING YOUR ART. Your pieces will find buyers in a short period of time that will be willing to pay the best price for it.

1.8 Personal image and branding as an artist

To be a professional artist, it is not enough to produce pieces of art. It's necessary to sell and earn money with them. You have to create an image of yourself as an artist, a professional brand and show the entire world what it is you do. You have to exist in the internet so that people can appreciate you, they can follow you in social media and stay in touch with you. Your work has to be showcased on the Internet and on specialized websites. Now a days, the first thing a potential buyer does when they like one of your pieces, is search your name and work on the Internet. If they can't find you on Wikipedia, they will probably expect to find you in any other web page like virtual art galleries, online auctions, newspaper sites and social media. If they can't find you in any of these websites, your work will probably not ignite the same interest as if it were. They will probably want to purchase it at the price of house decoration and not an art piece. I do not believe selling your work this way is what your goal. If you do not exist in the Internet as an artist, your art pieces are worth the same as any home ornament bought at a store. If your art is not on the Internet, it doesn't exist. If you don't exist as an artist, your work is worth only the price the material used to create it and your time. In this case you are an artisan and you will have to charge accordingly.

On the contrary, if your work can be found on the Internet, you are active on social media, if you participate in all sorts of cultural events and you showcase your work in a proper way, people will come up to you looking for the artist that you are. Obviously, they will want to purchase the work of a successful artist and not the work of an artisan no one has heard of. It's a process that begins from the creation of your brand as an artist and ends with the successful sales of your works of art. You can start slowly at first and see the first results in a few months. Doing the right thing and doing it properly is the only thing that guarantees the best results in life and in business. Same goes for your profession as an artist.

1.9 The multiplying effect of your works of art

When an artist produces a work of art, he or she uses a certain amount of materials in a specific amount of time. If the artist wants to win more money they can try to save purchasing materials at a cheaper store and optimize their process to finish the piece in a shorter period of time. Both ways are valid and efficient. I recommend paying attention to the cost of materials and the time you invest in finishing the pieces. There is one thing that really counts if you want to increase your revenue: The sales price. This is always valid and it works the same for a painting, a sculpture, a digital impression, porcelain and any other art form. In order to earn a lot of money in each transaction, you have to sell your work at the highest price possible. Guess which is the element that allows you to increase your prices? Your reputation and your fame as an artist are the only things that can increase their value.

Your success will not arrive by optimizing costs and time invested. The reputation and fame of an artist now a days is created with online presence, events, contests, auctions, marketing, public relations and interaction with fans and followers. These factors multiply the sales price and determine your success as a professional artist. If you want to make a living out of this you need to take care of these aspects and manage them in the best way possible as if you were A COMPANY.

CHAPTER 2

PREPARING THE TERRAIN

2.1 Production of 25 to 250 pieces of art

Whichever branch of art you decide to embark on, the first thing you need to do is have good stock of pieces to sell. Your products in this case are your pieces of art so: let's do it! My advice regarding the number of pieces to produce and the sizes are purely referential. They have a practical and logical commercial sense and they are meant to expand your market number of potential clients.

I invite you to carefully evaluate the situation making different decisions based on the type of artist you are, the amount of storage space you have and the way you see things. The important thing is that you take into consideration that you will need a large stock available at different sizes and prices. Remember, in this market if you don't have it, you can't sell it. To increase the amounts of potential buyers, you do not have to change your art or the style of your pieces. Try to get within reach of most of their pockets. Then you have to make sure your pieces fit in elevators and you also have to make sure they can fit the majority of wall space of all types of apartments and homes.

The only way of doing this is creating pieces of different sizes. You have to create very small pieces to very large pieces. That way you will be able to reach all types of clients, from those who live in small spaces and can pay lesser amount to those who can afford large pieces that can fit in larger spaces. I have met artists that only produce massive pieces as if their clients were large banks, multinational companies or royal families. This is not an ideal commercial strategy, at least not when you are first starting off as a professional artist.

I have also met artists than only produce small pieces because they focus on selling their work in artisan shops. This is also not ideal, because your sales depend on volume and you are missing out on selling your work to a portion of the market that is able to pay a lot more money for less pieces. These clients are surrounded by people with the same economic potential. So, if you are able to sell your work to his market it's a guarantee that your work will be seen by friends, clients, family members that could fall in love with your artistic style and could potentially acquire one of your pieces. You have to have available stock of all kinds of sizes and at different prices. In the future, when you become a more successful artist, you could focus on specific type of measurements. The ones you prefer or are more profitable for you.

Inventory and Pricing

After you have produced all your pieces you have to create an inventory. You must write down all the titles and exact measurements in centimeters and inches. Those are the most utilized metric systems. Then you should take high resolution professional photographs in each of your pieces. I recommend that you hire a professional photographer to get high quality pictures in which your work can be greatly appreciated. Art comes in through the eyes and if they are captured through the eye of a professional photographer there is no doubt you will find buyers. Do not underestimate the importance of this subject. Also, I suggest you take a picture of yourself beside your paintings and also take pictures of the details of each piece. You will need these pictures later for social media. Now that you have from 25 to 250 art pieces produced and inventoried you can set a price for them. I can't tell you what price to set for each piece, but I will give you basic tips about how to choose a minimum asking price for each of your items. The minimum asking price should be calculated with this simple equation:

MATERIALS
+
WORKING HOURS
+
YOUR FAME
+
YOUR ITEMS FAME
=
FINAL PRICE

In other words, your minimum asking price depends greatly on the price of the materials you have used plus the number of hours you put into creating it. There is no sense in selling an item for less than what it cost you to make it, especially when you are just starting your career as an artist. Then, you can add an additional amount proportional to the amount of fame you have as an artist.

If no one knows your name, you cannot use it to raise the asking price. Never sell your work at a very low price, even if you are just starting. It is better to maintain a higher price and offer generous discounts if necessary. People love the idea of buying something with a discount.

If you are not very known, your name might not help raise the price of an item. Nevertheless, if your piece has participated in an art show, if it has been exhibited in a good museum for a short amount of time next to the big names in history or it has been published in a book or a magazine, this could all help raise your asking price.

This equation helps you in an almost scientific way to determine the price of your work. I insist in recommending that you do not sell a piece for less than it cost you because it doesn't make sense. You must always charge for the price of your materials and the amount of time you put into making it. So, you already have a complete inventory, pictures, measurements and asking prices. It is not necessary that you complete all your works of art in order to continue. There are many points in this book that can be done at the same time, if and when you have the economic availability and time to advance.

I want to leave you with a very important concept: prepare the path so you can make a living off of your art, it is going to be difficult and it will take some time and a certain amount of money. There are no shortcuts and it will require investing some money. There are no ways in which you can do this quickly without any starting capital.

You can opt for going slow and steady while optimizing the necessary expenses, but you have to remember that a minimum investment will always be necessary.

2.2 Create your own web page: WWW.YOURNAME.COM

If you wish for people to find you when they do web searches, you have to create a web page that has information about yourself and you work as an artist. I recommend that your domain name has your complete name and surname followed by the word "art", "arte", "artist", "painter" or any other similar word that drives them to your site and everything you do. This is so they can not confuse you with anyone else and so you can easily find the available domain. You can do this for small amounts of money by purchasing a domain in www.godaddy.com and create a web page using www.wix.com.

Do not worry if you are not a web programmer. These portals were created for people like you and me who lack computer and programming skills. With a small investment of 100 USD and a few hours of work invested into doing this you can have your own web page in no time and finally exist in the Internet. Now a days any person that wants more information about you and your work will google you and read about you.

You have to upload several nice pictures of yourself in your webpage. I also suggest you write a short curriculum with every detail from where you studied to where you have exhibited our work. Do not forget to create the contact section with your email and phone number so that people know how to get in contact with you. Add special links to your social media pages so your fans can follow you. I recommend not to exaggerate anything you publish. Altering the information about certain contests or exhibitions can be damaging to your reputation and image. Only write the truth about what you publish and do it in a nice way.

Now a days, the information is accessible to anyone. If they are false or exaggerated in any way this can hurt your career. Throughout your career, your personality, your sincerity and the beauty of your work are the only things that will help you become successful as an artist. Never forget this.

Important tip

Pay close attention to the key words you use for the index of your web page in google search engines. The order in which they appear is decided by complex algorithms that depend on the quality of your information, the way you show it and the traffic that is generated by your webpage. It is really a delicate subject and extremely important. If you do not do this right, no one will find you on the internet. Even though platforms such as WIX are easy to use, I recommend you get an expert to do it. With a small investment, this person can analyze your web content and insert key words to optimize the way in which your page can be found on Google.

2.3 Print out business cards

No matter where you go, always take business cards with you. If you are at a public event, an exhibit, an auction or any other important event you can not only introduce yourself with a simple handshake. You must always hand in your business card. Simple and professional. It must have your contact information such as: phone number, WhatsApp, email, social media. I recommend you include one of your pieces on the back side of the business card. Make your business card truly beautiful so that no one will want to throw it away.

Your business card has to motivate potential buyers to want to look you up and connect with you on social media. It is the first step to make someone get to know you. Let your business card feed the curiosity of whoever receives it. Maybe not today or tomorrow, but sooner or later someone is going to be interested in what you do. Maybe that person could invite you to participate in an art show or even purchase one of your pieces. Do not underestimate the power of business cards. Remember, if you don't sell electric light bulbs or organic fertilizers, you sell emotions through your art. The emotion can begin with a simple business card.

2.4 Write an illustrated book

You are an artist, it is important that you create an illustrated book that has information of yourself and your pieces. It has to be a complete and extensive version of what you have already showcased on your webpage. It is a small investment and yet a bit complex because you have to hire someone to revise and correct that text and create a book cover. Also, you have to pay the costs of impression depending on the quantity of issues you print. I recommend to start with 25-30 issues.

This will be an excellent way of presenting yourself to art galleries, museum directors, etc. Also, you will be able to put them up for sale with your original signature in the first page and you will also use them as currency to pay some of the services such as photographers, editors, bloggers or influencers to promote your pieces. Art lovers love to receive autographed illustrated books. We will talk about this subject later on. You are probably in the beginning of your career as an artist and for this reason you will not have a high budget available to spend, but believe me that having your own illustrated book is important. The digital version as well as the printed version are a prestigious way to present yourself to the public. As an alternative, you could begin printing brochures that illustrate only specific pieces and a summarized biography. Its more accessible and yet still efficient. It will give you visibility but it will be less prestigious than an illustrated book. Do not worry, you can do this in another time.

2.5 Autographed printed pieces and lithographs

If you are a painter, photographer, digital artist or any type of artist that produces art that can be appreciated in a photograph, you have to create lithographs and impressions of your most successful pieces. It could be that more traditional collectors will not like them, but it is the cheapest form to get people to buy your art.

Most people do not have the money to invest in an original painting, but anyone can buy an autographed lithography. Keep in mind that your work can be at the reach of many art lovers. To sell signed lithographs or limited-edition photograph is the most profitable way to monetize an art piece. They represent, in some cases, the greatest form of revenue for you. If you only sell an oil painting over 40x40 cm canvas at 2,500 USD, which is rather high, you will be making a profit of 2,300 USD if you subtract the materials and time you used. If you produce 200 lithographs of this same painting, you will pay maximum 20 dollars for each one for a total of 4,000 USD of investment. If you sell them little by little numbered and autographed by you at a reasonable price of 120USD each, you will earn 20,000 USD. Yes, you read correctly, I wrote twenty thousand dollars of net revenue in a single painting.

Imagine what you could earn producing lithographs of all your major art work. You could sell them on your website, in galleries and even in specialized stores. You can also sell some of them in art exhibits and in events in which you are participating. Even if you take the absurd decision of focusing on selling lithographs and to stop selling your art, you could still make a lot of money.

You need to keep in mind that the importance of the lithograph is represented by two factors. The first one is that you can transport or send them wherever you need with little investment and effort. This permits you to organize your art exhibits in a simpler form whenever the space or price is not agreeable. For example, in fairs or places where you don't have much space or traffic and for that reason you cannot transport your original works, it generates an elevated cost that wouldn't make sense. Remember, what you want to transmit with your art is emotion. A lithograph can do exactly this almost the same as any original piece. Second, you can use them as currency and exchange them for any service you require. For instance, you can pay bloggers and influencers with signed lithographs instead of giving them money to publish any content you require. Not everyone will accept this as payment, but in many cases they will and that will help you save a lot of money. You will pay 125 USD in services with a lithograph that cost you 20 USD to make. This also represents a decent profit. It's better that it is in your pocket instead of someone else's. Your pieces and lithographs may not spark everyone's interest, but many professionals will prefer to receive them as a form of payment than to lose a potential client. Take this into consideration and suggest your books or pieces as a first payment option.

If I'm not a painter, what can I do instead of lithographs?

You can play with this idea and find a creative solution. There are many options depending on your art. For instance, you can produce a signed limited series of 100 issues in any of these branches:

- Mosaics
- Sculptures
- Printed photographs
- Porcelain
- Drawings
- Silver
- Digital art impression
- Wood carving
- Art with textiles
- Glass fusing

The importance thing is that all pieces be identifiable as your own, not just because they have your signature. Also, remember that the final goal of this limited production is to earn profit selling them to clients with less budget to spend. If an original piece is worth 5,000 USD, a small replica of an original piece can be sold at 500 USD. As long as you recover the cost of your time and materials. Art is not only a series of original large pieces, it also consists of a series of signed and authenticated reproductions by the artist. The world is not only full of art collectors with lots of money, it is also full of people with less disposable income. They represent a great potential source of income because they represent the majority of the population. Original and expensive pieces are for those who can afford them and a limited release of smaller replicas are for the rest. The smaller market is a market with lots of potential and its worth to consider it as a target. It's important to focus in all the potential buyers that exist and you have to offer them options that could adapt to their budget.

2.6 Create your own Wikipedia page

It is not necessary to be famous to have presence in Wikipedia, it's an independent non-profit website that has the purpose of disclosing unbiased information about any topic. In fact, anyone can freely offer their service and write an article on a topic that is not mentioned in the page. It's very important that you appear on Wikipedia as an artist. Write an article about your life and profession, be impartial and objective, do not use promotional or flattering messages. Write as if you want to report yourself fairly. In no way try to promote your work because they would not approve this article. If this is your first time writing on this platform, it will probably take a little longer for them to accept you article. They will investigate about you and if they find your website, your social media profile and in some cases a newspaper article that talks about your work, the approval of your article will be easier. If you do not know how to do it, ask for help from someone who knows how to handle the issue. It's a very non-expensive and very effective method. Being on Wikipedia is very important because ordinary people believe that only famous people are there. This will give you more prestige, visibility and credibility.

2.7 Create your social media profiles

It may be the case that you don't particularly enjoy being on social media, but if you're not using these pages, then you practically don't exist and your visibility reduces enormously. For an artist nowadays, it is important to at least be on Instagram and Facebook. They are perfect platforms to constantly showcase your art, be in touch with your fans and followers and to promote certain events in which you showcase your work. Do not use social media to sell immediately because it looks unprofessional. Online profiles don't work as online stores. You could better utilize your social media platforms as a way of connecting with your fans and to constantly deliver high quality content and guide them to the places where your work is available to buy. To properly sell your pieces, you have to use professional channels like online stores, virtual or real galleries and specialized online marketplaces. This gives you a touch of credibility and prestige that are important in your profession. This will also maintain your reputation with professional gallerists that have committed to invest in marketing your pieces.

You will not lose sales, in fact quite the contrary, you will gain prestige and more time to dedicate to creating new pieces. I recommend you sell them directly only to those people you know personally and those who are already clients of yours and huge fans. You can also sell them directly to clients you meet in a fair or an art exhibit if and when you respect the pricing and marketing policy you have negotiated with your gallerists and art dealers. Maintaining your high reputation with these professionals is very important if you want to grow as a professional artist. Direct sales yes, but do it with criteria and respecting the rules.

Another interesting social network is LinkedIn, it is very important if you create commissioned art or in digital form. Otherwise it is just one more cover letter. It is useful but not indispensable. What is essential is that you have your YouTube channel. You can use it to publish short videos of your work that is in progress. These are very popular with fans. You can also post videos of interviews you've done, videos of exhibitions or contests in which you have participated. You can also post short videos of yourself while you're creating your art or videos in which you teach special art techniques. Being a teacher with students interested in learning your techniques, gives you prestige and value while improving your reputation as an artist.

2.8 Create two databases

Client databases represent a very important and strategic tool for the sales of any company. Constantly updating is a very good way of keeping it useful. Not everyone understands the importance and potential of the results that are obtained with a properly updated database and for this reason very few people use it correctly. It is ideal to send discounts and special promotions directly to the people that are interested in your art.

It works perfectly when interacting directly with customers and potential buyers sending them quality information or digital gifts on special occasions such as birthdays and Christmas. It's the way to market your products at a good price and in an efficient way. For this reason, it is important that you take advantage of this very useful tool.

Create two databases and keep it constantly updated. If you use it properly they'll help you earn a lot of money throughout your career as an artist. They represent a very important resource for your business.

The first database has to be about your potential clients and art lovers. At first, it could be a short list but if you update it every week, you will see after a few short months, you will have been able to grow it exponentially. You can contact them each time you have to present a new piece of art or any special event you might be participating in.

Don't send frequent sales and promotions because they can grow tired of receiving your emails and categorize you as spam. Only talk about new pieces or cultural events related to your work. Send useful information and share high quality content that they would like to see and share with their friends.

The day they become ready to purchase one of your pieces, they will do so because every potential buyer matures at due time if they are stimulated enough. Forcing it will only make them uncomfortable and stay away from you. Remember, one of your professional missions is to draw more and more people to your art.

Please, keep in mind that this strategy is my personal opinion. If you do not agree and think that your audience is interested in constantly receiving information about your work, go ahead and do it. No one knows art lovers more than you, but remember that persuasive publicity can make clients uncomfortable.

The second database has to include people who can help you market your pieces. Divide it into categories for gallerists, art teachers, influencers, bloggers, youtubers, event planners, museum directors, graphic designers, digital copiers and any other category related to your type of art. You are going to use this database daily.

Keep it updated, it will allow you take action with more accuracy. This is essential for all businesses. You might probably think that it's not that important to create two databases for your career as an artist. Updating and storing and properly using the information in your databases is essential for anyone who makes a living selling pieces to clients.

It represents a powerful tool that will allow you to always sell more pieces of art in less time and with less effort. You will create a community of fans that will be happy to be invited to events or be informed about any new piece you are working on.

If databases weren't that important, there would be no companies and professionals that sell segmented databases. There would also be no successful companies that invest thousands of dollars to increase databases and manage them correctly.

They are profitable and efficient and whoever uses them correctly knows this very well. The importance of a good database in undoubtable. Start building your own database as soon as possible. We have reached the end of the chapter and you have learned to prepare the terrain for the bases of your career as an artist. If we were talking about agriculture, we would have prepared the soil to be ready for the planting of the seeds.

Shall we start planting seeds and knocking on doors?

2.9 Create signed certificates of authenticity for your pieces

It doesn't matter what type of art you sell, you have to sell your pieces accompanied by a certificate of authenticity with your personal seal and signed. It is very important and clients love it. Also, it's not expensive. Design a certificate with a specific logo that represents you or your personal brand. Print several in special paper and have them ready for each sale. I recommend that you hand write the name of the piece, the date it was made and your signature. Do not use bad quality paper or an improvised design because this will also represent your image, your brand and your company as an artist. Do it well, or don't do it at all.

My father used to say that if people can replicate paintings they can also replicate certificates of authenticity, and perhaps at some moment you might believe it's useless to make them. Remember, it's a fast and accessible detail that adds quality to your work. It generates a sense of credibility. I always ask for a certificate of authenticity whenever I buy a piece. I always request it in case someday in the future I decide to sell the piece, it will be easier to find a good buyer with a certificate of authenticity. A certificate of authenticity helps sell a piece at a better price.

2.10 Chapter Summary

- Produce an initial stock
- Photograph your art and create an inventory
- Define sales prices
- Create an artist website
- Make beautiful business cards
- Create and print illustrated books
- Print lithographs or limited series pieces
- Create your Wikipedia profile
- Create your own certificates of authenticity for each piece
- Create social media profiles (Instagram, Facebook, Twitter)
- Create two databases

Chapter 3

PROMOTION AND MARKETING OF YOUR ART

3.1 Contact art galleries

Art galleries, both regular and digital represent a strategic and important point of sale. Start negotiating with them as soon as possible. They will charge you a commission whenever they sell one of your pieces, but it's better that you earn a percentage of a good sale than earn nothing from zero sales. They are, next to contemporary art museums, the best way to showcase your art. It's in galleries where big clients and art collectors can be found.

Maybe they won't make you rich, but you will earn prestige when one of your pieces is showcased in galleries. Write a former cover letter in which you introduce yourself and send them via email to every gallery you can find. Include nice photographs of your most important pieces along with your website link. Do not mention prices in the cover letter, mention all the places and contests you have showcased your art and also include art school information if applicable. It's important you also write something about your work and type of art you create. What is your inspiration and what you want to communicate with your art.

Don't forget to include your social media profiles and your Wikipedia page. Also indicate that you not only sell original pieces but you also sell lithographs, printed art and limited series pieces for all types of collectors. Mention you have autographed books and all type of material available, both physical and digital. Indicate that you are available to meet with them virtually if necessary. It's important that they see you as a professional.

Always be prepared and available to formally discuss the terms and conditions if they were to showcase your art in their gallery. If you can send presentations in physical form, top galleries would take notice. I recommend you use the postal service with a high-quality leaflet directed to the gallery owner. Your mail will stand out and it will arrive straight to the right person. It's an expensive method but it is efficient and precise.

3.2 Publish your work in online art classifieds

Online classifieds are dedicated to the sale of works of art in which collectors and artists unite their interests.

They are ideal for publishing advertisements and putting all your works for sale. They are usually very cheap and charge only a percentage when a sale is made.

They don't have a lot of traffic like social networks, but their users are people who are interested in art, therefore your target market. They are visitors with a high conversion rate. It's important to be present in these portals because famous collectors are usually using these platforms to discover new talent and emerging artists.

I recommend you publish your works at quite high prices so that you have a higher negotiation margin. It is always good to give a client a good piece and the feeling that they have obtained it for less that it was worth. You can easily manage this because you create your works, you choose the process, you negotiate with the buyer. Never forget that everyone loves discounts.

3.3 Publish your work on generic online classifieds

In these pages, not all the audience is interested in art as well as in the case of specialized classifieds, but it is important to be in them and write ads correctly, because their indexing in search engines is excellent. It is likely that if you google your first and last name followed by the word art or sell, you will find an advertisement for them before your website.

It is the power to know exactly how google searches work. Use the well-known classifieds platforms as much as you can because that are free and have great potential. Perhaps most of your sales do not come through this medium but anyone who searches for you on the internet will find you everywhere. This increases your credibility, fame and importance as an artist, and the prices of your works will not be unattended.

3.4 Sell your work on eBay

eBay is one of the largest online sales platforms in the world. Due to its nature, it is highly frequented by collectors of all types of articles and products. Many people check if you exist as an artist and if there are works of yours for sale. Many people also use eBay to check if you are for real and to check how high your prices are. Always keep two or three pieces for sale at a high price. It is an important showcase and you need it to defend the value well in the other sales channels. Sometimes, you may even get the pleasant surprise of making a sale on this platform.

3.5 Use Influencers

Influencers today are widely used to promote products and services. Even the largest multinational companies. The power of your audience's reach is beyond question.

With their content posts on Instagram, or Facebook, they reach a very large audience and are ideal for promoting artists and works of art as well. Choose to work with those who have a level of content that is appropriate and culturally compatible with your artwork. If an influencer deals with subjects that are very far from the art theme, he will probably have followers that are not really interested in buying your art and your money will be poorly invested. Reach an agreement with several influencers, promoting your work or exhibitions.

Remember that they are very flexible to negotiate prices for their publications because they have no material cost. They also accept products in exchange. I recommend paying them with autographed lithographs or very small original pieces in case the influencer is famous and has many followers. Always try to exchange your lithographs or limited series work as payment first or a combination of both alternatives. I recommend you do your research because there are tons of influencers and there are always those who would accept a lithograph in exchange for a post.

There are also many pages dedicated to each type of art on Instagram and Facebook which have a large following and are owned by people who love art. It is likely that they will accept a small piece in exchange for a little publicity among their fans.

3.6 Use bloggers

Bloggers are people who write their opinions on specific topics, sending their articles to a group of followers who appreciate its content. They're usually people who are characterized by talking about topics of a specific niche such as cooking, business, art, etc. Identify bloggers who are willing to write about your career as an artist and your work and negotiate with them.

Sometimes they will do it for free or in exchange for a nice lithograph. Some of them are very successful people who have a fairly high number of followers. Perhaps it won't be easy to get their attention at first, but later on this could be possible. In the meantime, dedicate yourself to negotiating with those who are most available to you and who are willing to publish content about your work. It is an excellent way to create an audience and show people your works. It goes without saying that you are just looking for bloggers covering content related to art and culture. Trust me, it's not worth working with people whose followers aren't interested in the content being published. It would be a waste of time and money.

3.7 Use YouTubers

YouTubers are influencers who publish content on their channel through videos produced by themselves. There are thousands and different, dealing with topics of all kinds. It would be great to create a video where the YouTuber interviews you and asks you about your life and your work.

The videos in which the YouTuber talks about you and your art are also very good, but he has to be a very prepared person on the subject or he would bore his followers and you would lose credibility as a result of that. You should not only look for an art YouTuber, but someone who has an audience that may be interested in the subject. It is a waste of money to show art videos to people who are not interested. Furthermore, it is inappropriate to use an influencer whose profile is culturally far from your art. Better that the video and its content be something sincere and credible.

To summarize, the content is going to look like just another advertisement and it's not the goal in this case. You can also invite YouTubers to your exhibitions, event or auctions in which your works are involved. A video may be directly next to a work of yours would be an excellent means of advertising. Many YouTubers will be happy to provide their services to you, in exchange for money, lithographs, original pieces or a combination of all three. Always remember that your work, your autographed books and your lithographs are an excellent currency to pay for promotional services.

Take the possibility of learning how to create your own videos and post them on your own YouTube channel seriously. If you do it right, it's a great way to keep in touch with art lovers. The same rule also applies as in other social networks. SHARE ONLY HIGH-QUALITY CONTENT, that adds value to your image as a person and as a professional artist.

3.8 Contact art critics and journalists

Both represent a hard to reach category. Even more so if you are taking your first steps in the art world. But why not try it? Nowadays all the contacts you need are on the Internet and it doesn't cost anything to write an email or send them a nice letter of introduction. Worst case scenario, they won't read it, but sooner or later they may be missing work material or topics to write about and they will surely check in your database or emails.

It is better that you get used to dealing with art critics and journalists in the sector as soon as possible because they are the ones that have a lot of influence on the information being published on the subject. It is a very small niche and they are the ones that influence the price of your work and people's general opinion about you.

Earning their esteem and trust means that you have important professionals who support you and your work. Many of them also write in digital newspapers and with their articles they will leave an important mark on the Internet that speaks well of you and your art.

This news appears in Google search engines so do not underestimate the importance of a well-indexed article that talks about you on the internet. Once you have several critics or journalists in your database, always formally invite them to your artistic events. They live on it, and will be honored to participate. It also always includes the ones that don't like you very much.

They may not like your art or what you are doing in this period of your professional life, but they probably like you as a person. In business, rejections are never directed at you, they are always professional and are directed at the finished work. The important thing is that people talk about you. Your work cannot be liked by everyone. What matters is that a small part of art lovers like them.

What really counts is having your group of admirers keeping in touch with them and taking actions that increase the number of followers on your social networks. You always have to work with appropriate marketing strategies and high-quality content.

3.9 Collaborate with your fellow colleagues

You may have never seen it this way, but both emerging and established artists can help each other to seek more visibility and followers. They can collaborate for free in many ways, benefiting each other. One option would be to publish content about one or more colleagues on your social networks and have them do the same with your work. They can interview each other in turn and publish the content in both their profiles.

Photos and videos can be taken while producing works simultaneously or with four hands. Your colleagues' followers and fans are mostly art lovers and they will probably appreciate your creations too. They can also organize joint exhibitions between two or more artists, sharing the expenses and involving many more acquaintances.

Your friendships, along with those of the other artists participating will result in a much wider audience. It is a very agreeable and democratic way of creating interest around art. Consider other artists as colleagues and not as direct competition. Someone who can define him or herself as your "competitor" should be able to lure clients and market share away from you. I highly doubt that a fellow artist can do that. On the contrary, a colleague's client can perhaps be encouraged to buy something of yours too if he or she comes to like one of your pieces. Your colleagues will never pose a threat to your sales. They are precious companions with whom you can build a powerful team of people that join forces and share their loyal following. It's a win-win situation. You all need visibility and collaboration when it comes to organizing an art event. Send your colleagues a proposal and you shall see that lots of them would be honored to participate.

3.10 Art intermediaries

Basically, they are people who do the same work as a gallery, but in a different way. Perhaps more informal and sometimes without having physical space to exhibit your art work. This doesn't not mean that they're not effective, on the contrary, they are people who do it through their contacts and public relations platforms. Their database is very valuable. They only approach people who are interested in collecting art. They don't send emails, but they call or write their contacts personally. I have seen some bring artwork to my home just to display. They are very effective at targeting because they know their customers very well and know exactly what each one of them is looking for in terms of preferences.

They are rare to find but if you search properly, you can find them. Formally reach an agreement with them and write down the sales terms and conditions of your pieces. They have a very efficient method and are in contact with many art collectors. Each time you find one, try to work together to sell your work and pay them good commissions. Paying commissions is never a bad investment. It's always a good investment plus, you pay commission only when they actually sell one of your pieces.

3.11 Chapter Summary

- Write a letter to introduce yourself to all the online and offline art galleries you know
- Put your work for sale in specialized art portals
- Publish your work in national and local generic classifieds
- Showcase your work on eBay
- Write to all Facebook or Instagram influencers who publish content that is compatible with yours to negotiate advertising spaces on their accounts
- Write to all related YouTubers to create quality video content about yourself
- Contact as many bloggers as possible to interview and write about you
- Learn to collaborate with your fellow artists to increase audience as well as sharing expenses when organizing events
- Arrange with art intermediaries to sell your work using their contacts

CHAPTER 4

SALES AND EVENTS

4.1 Participate in Auctions

Art auctions represent a very effective and prestigious way of selling your work. Therefore, it is ideal for you to participate whenever possible. Although your pieces may not always sell at the price you were hoping for, auctions are a great way to meet collectors, fellow colleagues, artists and everyone involved in the art world. Constantly moving in this environment and increasing your database represents the engine of your activity as an art seller.

Remember that you cannot only dedicate yourself to produce, but you must also sell. Never neglect this matter. Without good contacts there are no sales and therefore, no incoming revenue. Without income you cannot pay your expenses and then you might have to search for an alternative profession and abandon your beloved craft. It is not advisable to abandon your sales strategies because your income as an artist depends on them. I have met artists who do not participate in auctions because the offers do not always reach the asking price. They ignore the real reason for which an artist participates in an auction. It's not just about the money you make from the sale. It's all about the exposure.

It's about meeting people, gaining credibility and improving your artistic curriculum. It is very important to be present at these events. In addition, this will also help you stay updated on market trends, average asking prices and technical information such as the average size of paintings that actually sell. It will be beneficial for you to be aware of these commercial topics.

Even though as an artist you perhaps might be more interested in the creative side of art, you also need to be able to sell your work. If not, you'll soon find yourself in the position of searching for other sources of income. I understand that you prefer to dedicate yourself to think and produce art, but without sales there is no income.

Never forget it. I have also met artists who do not even try to participate in auctions, convinced that they are not famous enough or well known. Do not worry about that. You always have to believe in yourself and your jobs. In the art world this is very important. No one will believe in you if you don't believe in yourself. Apply for as many auctions as you can.

They are free opportunities to promote your brand as an artist and your work as an art seller. Also, why they should reject your work if they are beautiful and come from an artist with a webpage, Wikipedia profile and an artist that constantly showcases their work in galleries, art classifieds and marketplaces. Are you now understanding why I wrote the first three chapters? I'm sure you now have a much clearer concept of what I'm talking about.

4.2 Participate in Art Contests

Participating in art contests is equally important as auctions, for all the reasons I mentioned in the previous section. What is not really that important is to win. With this I am not saying that the first place in an art contest is not advantageous for you because of course it could be.

The prize itself does not make you sell more of your work, what helps you sell is your set of contacts and how you move within the art world. If I were an artist, I would rather focus on constantly participating in as many contests as I can, regardless of whether they ever reward me. The real reward is to sell your work not to win medals. I know very talented artists who have won prestigious competitions but have ended up abandoning their art career. A former school mate participated in a biennial and won a contest with a remarkable piece. It is a self-portrait where she is covered by a red veil, and of course she found a buyer immediately.

I do not know how happy the owner of this painting is today, knowing that the painter is no longer dedicated to art. On the other hand, I know artists who have never won an award and are very successful in terms of sales. As I told you before, what counts is the image of an active and determined artist that has the best sales results in the long term. If you never win an art contest, do not worry. Participate anywhere you can with pride and determination. Sales will surely follow.

4.3 Organize exhibits

An art exhibition is as important for an artist as a match is for a football player. It is the most traditional way of showing your artwork to the public. So, I will not write more about how important they are, but it is worth advising you on how to organizing them while minimizing costs and maximizing results. In the previous chapter, we discussed the idea of sharing exhibitions with other artists, to save expenses and involve more people who participate in the event. In case you want to organize exhibitions where you are the only artist, I recommend at least involving other artists with whom you can create more audience and mutual benefits.

You can put together an exhibition in conjunction with wine cellars, fine food producers, gourmet, food stores, restaurants, craft stores, travel agencies and many more businesses. It all depends on your creativity and your contacts. It's a bonus for all guests as well, who can be introduced and offered not only art, but also food, travel, discounts and more. Another option to exhibit your work is in fine restaurants or in boutique stores. Depending on the space available, you can leave some of your paintings or pieces there with your name and contact information under each of them.

Many entrepreneurs will be happy to temporarily place them in their place of business. This special touch of artistic culture greatly stimulates their clients and the best entrepreneurs know this very well. There is no limit to all the ways there are to exhibit works of art with a relatively low investment. You will be able to work based on your contacts. Remember one thing, these are fortuitous occasions where you will be able to talk to people and collect as many contacts as possible to enrich your database.

4.4 Participate in cultural events

There are many cultural events that may be organized in your city or in nearby towns, wherever you are in the world, you have to try to exhibit your art in most of them. They are not necessarily art events, but this is not that important. There is always a small space or corner where you can display your work. You can showcase your art in a wine and/or food tasting. You can do it in a high fashion show, during a concert, political meetings, electoral elections. If you network creatively, you can grow your database exponentially. Also, you will see that there are dozens of people who organize events for their businesses every week, and who would be honored and delighted to give you space to participate as an artist.

Despite how complicated it is to become an expert collector, art is something that fascinates many people. Everyone has respect for it, even the ones who show little interest. Any business event is more respectable if it is accompanied by an art exhibit. No one will say this to you, but believe me, this is how it is. If you're trying to get into an ethnic crafts or specially packaged canned foods exhibition, perhaps not everyone will agree with that. Not everyone will immediately take to the idea because it might seem like a street vendor stall or feel out of context. But if you do it with works of art and you are professional, you are on the internet, you expose frequently, you have a website, you are on Wikipedia, this is where the music changes. Everyone has respect for that and will be honored to enrich the event with an art exhibition. It does not matter if the event organizer likes your work or not.

Anyone would gladly accept this wonderful opportunity. The hosts will personally introduce you to all their guests, which is a great source of contacts for your database. It is also important that you are properly dressed in accordance to the theme or event during which you will have to behave in a professional manner. Start conversations with whomever you can, be discreet and don't try to sell to anyone. This is not the right time or place. These types of events are purely for exposure.

Sales can be made in a more appropriate time. Many guests will be delighted to meet you and admire your creations and hear about them directly from the artist. An artist whose profile can be found in Wikipedia, has a professional website, charming business cards, autographed lithographs, a proper CV of contests and exhibitions in which he or she has participated, a generous smile, a nice inventory available for sale and many future career plans. This is what people are interested in when buying art work. They want to take it and proudly show it to their friends, mentioning where you were showcased, where they met you, how talented and friendly you are and the great career you have as an artist. They will advertise though word of mouth, which is the most sincere and effective form of marketing for any type of seller and product.

4.5 Raise funds for charity, "The multiplier effect"

It is very important to help others and donate whenever you can, whatever your profession may be. It doesn't matter how much you give; what matters is that you do it with intention and in proportion to what you earn. Remember that a small contribution is very valuable to people that are in need.

Do not be sorry if your contributions seem low, because every bit helps. Only you know what you can do to help others. Remember that it is easier for you to contribute with charitable foundations and causes. The artist represents a money multiplier when it comes to raising funds for donations. In fact, you don't always have to donate money. You can also auction off a piece and donate the entirety of the collected funds. Maybe the materials cost you very little money, therefore it would only consist of a small investment. With the multiplier effect you have as an artist, you can donate much more.

A couple of brush strokes and signature on a canvas can be transformed into a much larger contribution. This is what I call the multiplier effect. Also, remember that buyers are more generous if they are buying a work of yours, when they are aware of the fact that the funds will be donated to those less fortunate. I know many artists who do it and feel very happy because it.

The most successful ones even have private foundations that are responsible for raising funds for those who need help. Others carry out small works on cardboard or napkins monthly so that they can be bought by people with all kinds of budgets. In this matter, anyone can participate and contribute. Other artists go to orphanages to entertain children with art. Still others visit convicts and recovering drug addicts and offer free classes. Everyone does what they can and it's great. I recommend you periodically organize a fundraiser using your social networks to promote your artwork. As I mentioned before, you can also auction off your pieces any chance you can and invite your followers to participate in such events. Most of them would be honored to contribute. This is also the MULTIPLYING EFFECT of an artist.

Remember, if you have a certain number of followers and fans, big or small, they admire and appreciate you and your work. They would love to participate in your charitable initiatives. It's a great responsibility and that is why I recommend that you do it. Making profit and participating in these events is always a good thing. This will also help you become a more known artists and be appreciated by the public. The appreciation and esteem of your fans increases greatly when they know that you regularly support charitable causes. That being said, I suggest you not do it only for this reason. You have an entire book that instructs you in how to increase your sales. Do not do charity just to seek your own interests. Silently enjoy this indirect benefit and only help others out of a sense of solidarity. It is the right thing to do and remember, the more successful you are, the more you can help those in need with your work.

4.6 How to charge

How do you plan to charge your work? The first answer is obviously cash. Nevertheless, you should not limit you charging options. There are several alternatives when the first option is not feasible. You have to think beforehand about offering payment methods for those who buy something remotely, for instance. You have to present your clients with options.

PayPal

This is the most popular online payment platform up to date. Opening an account is free and immediate. You can use other alternatives similar to PayPal as long as you have verified that they can transfer money directly to your bank account. Other platforms you can use are the following: PAYONEER, AMAZON PAY, GOOGLE PAY, APPPLE PAY, SKRILL. Opening an account on each of these platforms is free and takes a few minutes. Having these payments options available is free and it gives you an advantage when it comes to closing a good sale.

Credit card

If you are in an art exhibition and someone wants to buy your work, chances are they will not carry cash or a checkbook. Potential clients would most likely carry a credit card. This form of payment is available to almost anyone. It is extremely important that you can accept it as a form of payment. There are portable devices that allow a smartphone or tablet to become a Point of Sale (POS) to accept payments with the main cards on the market. Investigate which bank offers this service in your country and get it as soon as possible. It is very important.

Installment payments

This is a good option for those clients who do not have credit cards and cannot pay cash up front. If possible, make them give you a post-dated check for each payment they owe you. You can offer a flexible short month payment for those pieces that are less expensive. For pieces that are more expensive, you can extend the term.

I recommend that you do not extend the payment term to more than two years. In case the client doesn't have a checkbook, you can also offer a payment in installments. The decision to deliver the piece before or after they finish paying you is entirely up to you. When signing the payment in installments contract, always charge an up-front payment of at least 10%. I know receiving a payment in installments is not the most comfortable situation for any artist, but remember that there is not much risk in these transactions which is worth considering. It's better to be flexible than to lose a sale because of a lack of payment options.

Exchange

Another viable option would be to exchange your piece with product or services you would need. For example, if you want to sell a piece to the owner of a wine cellar, an agreeable alternative would be to accept payment with wine products. It would be convenient for him and he will surely appreciate your flexibility.

The same goes for any other type of client. Evaluate each client whenever it is worth it to exchange products/services instead of money. Remember, you can always use the products exchanged to your benefit or distribute or resell them to your friends and/or family. You could also resell them on the Internet and in case of perishable products, you can negotiate delivery terms and conditions that could permit you to consume them comfortably. Do not underestimate the power of using this exchange as a tool for efficient negotiations.

I suggest you use it at a last resort, but do not think this option is any less important. In my entire career as an entrepreneur, I can assure you that thanks to the exchange of good and services I have recovered almost 20% of sales I was about to lose. I used to lose some sales before learning this technique. Most of the sales that fall through are because the buyer did not agree to the form of payment. If you wish to increase your sales and defend your price without lowering it too much, you have to be open and flexible when it comes to charging. Prepare to receive payments in any way possible in order to increase sales.

4.7 How can I earn money while my career is taking off?

I can imagine that in more than one occasion while reading this book, you have asked yourself how you are going to pay your monthly expenses while your career is taking off. In other words, you might be wondering how you could support yourself while putting into practice everything you are learning in this book.

The answer is simple and you decide which alternative to choose. The first option is that you look for a part-time job while dedicating your free time to creating works of art and marketing them as I have mentioned in this book. It might slow you down on your path to achieving your dream, but it is also important to pay your bills first. There is no way to avoid this.

The second option would be to dedicate yourself to one of the activities, which represent simple and effective ways to earn money with your artistic talent:

Freelancer

There are websites, where there are many clients who need to carry out a project and are looking for an artist. You can carefully explore all the available proposals and apply for the ones you like. They do not pay much but they are effective and allow you to gradually acquire a fixed clientele that will rehire you every time they need your services. On these sites, there is a lot of competition from other artists, so it is important to present interesting offers and maintain good communication with everyone. Two of the most popular sites among artists are: peopleperhour.com and upwork.com

Sell online prints

Nowadays it is possible to sell prints of your work on different Internet pages. When a customer buys one, they are in charge of producing it and sending it to its recipient. They only charge a commission while you decide the sale's price of each piece. It's a nice way to monetize with your drawings, even when you already earn money as a traditional artist. It's not difficult to manage multiple works of art on different accounts so I highly recommend this method. You only have to set it up properly and the rest comes automatically without the need for you to dedicate more time or effort.

Offer classes or courses

It is a great way to earn extra money. You can do it online especially if you work using digital media creating a webpage and selling your classes on social networks. You can also do it offline. There are many people who want to learn to draw, paint, sculpt and any other technique. You will decide what to teach and how to do it, adapting to each student and the time you have available.

Carry our commissioned work

Interacting with the client and making commissioned art is a great way to earn money, at least while you're still working on your career to take off permanently. I know this is probably not what you are looking for in your career but remember that your priority at this time is to pay your expenses until you start reaping the fruits of your work. It's something you can do temporarily until necessary.

4.8 How long before I obtain results?

This is a million-dollar question and there is no way to get an accurate answer. What you have to accept is that it may take several months for the fruits of your labor to materialize.

That's why it's necessary to have alternative sources of income that allow you to pay your expenses in the meantime. There is no way to speed up this process because it is complex. It requires perseverance, patience, a good attitude and self-confidence.

You are talented, and producing beautiful work while marketing them in the right way. You have to wait for the fruits to ripen before you can harvest them.

There is no way you can push this process without spending a lot of money on marketing, advertising, events, exhibitions and travel.

If you have these resources, you can decide to invest them, but otherwise in the first three chapters you have read all the steps that must be followed to optimize your strategies as a salesperson.

How long you will be able to keep on making a living off of your art will depend on many factors such as: where you live, lifestyle choices that require certain spending behaviors and of course your type of art. To give you an idea, generally speaking, you can achieve surprising results in less than a year if you use the adequate sales strategies.

4.9 Chapter Summary

- Participate in as many art auctions as you can
- Apply for all possible art contests
- Frequently organize exhibitions, preferably organized with collaboration from fellow artists
- Participate in cultural events and showcase your work wherever possible.
- Frequently organize and participate in charity fundraisers
- Sign up for PayPal and the vast majority of online payment platforms.
- If you need extra income, find out which is the best among the available options. The one that best matches your time flexibility and art style
- Teach art classes or courses
- Work on commissioned art

CHAPTER 5

RECOMMENDATIONS AND BEHAVIOR

Why this chapter?

As I said at the beginning of the book, I will not talk about art style and techniques nor have I covered issues that might help with your inspiration. These are topics that go beyond the purpose of this book. It must also be said that I am not trained in psychology, nor am I an art critic or artist. Any matter related to art, personal motivation and artistic inspiration I leave to others who are experts in these fields. I dare not cover this subject matter because it is very likely that I am wrong and this would harm you as an artist and myself as a writer. However, I remind you that I am an entrepreneur and an art collector. I know how this sector works and how things are sold. I know how art is sold and what buyers are usually looking for. I know this because I am an avid art lover and collector. I buy works of art that I admire and can afford and I constantly talk to people who share my passion for art even if I don't work in this world. I know what a passionate person is looking for, I know what a speculator is looking for and I know what any person looks for when they buy a work of art. All the advice you will read in this chapter are strictly personal opinions. It may be that you don't agree with all of them, or some of them may not be suitable for your type of art or personality. Reflect carefully based on your style and professional profile and you will know which advice is useful to you and which is not.

5.2 Speaking of your clothing

You probably won't agree with what I have to say about this topic or you might not be interested in advice about clothing. Do not fret, this is in no way a form of criticism and it is not essential that you follow this. You can be a successful artist by dressing any way you like. It's only a personal opinion about what I see in events. I would love to help you consider your clothing more as a work uniform than as a chosen style.

Remember that in life, THEY TREAT YOU AS THEY SEE YOU. It may seem unfair, but it's the truth. Dressing sharply at your events greatly improves your image towards potential customers. This is extremely important since they are people who are probably there to buy art. Selling is your only purpose at that moment and your clothes represent a sort of work uniform. I highly doubt that a manager of a multinational company or a lawyer always wears a jacket and tie.

They do it because they have to and it is for the same reason that you also respect certain protocols that help you as a professional. At work, the best way to dress is the one that helps optimize sales and performance. Dressing up doesn't make you a better professional or a better person, but it does influence the opinions others have of you as a professional. If you think that the opinion of others about how you dress does not matter, just remember who signs the checks to pay for your work. It is necessary for everyone to see the best version of you.

Your appearance, your personality and your artist image must be so bright that it can reach to illuminate your work and add value to it. Your work is only a reflection of your talent, the price depends on how you present them to the public. It doesn't really matter how much your clothes cost or how formal you look. You are an artist and your clothes can be part of the persona you created. What does matter is dressing decently. Man or woman, you have to use clothing in good condition and are presentable. I also recommend avoiding being too sexy because this could become counterproductive.

Remember, at events you want to network as much as possible and dressing inappropriately can make you unapproachable. Nowadays it is possible to find nice affordable clothing. It's better for an artist to present themselves as brilliant, extroverted and sharply dressed. In other times, artists did not have access to the salons and world events. The possibility of participating in these events was not even available to artists of Van Gogh's caliber. They painted to sell to the wealthy while socializing with the poor. Today, thanks to modern changes in society, all this is possible. You have to take advantage of this situation. Use your image and clothing to create a character that sells many works of art. Create an excellent brand that talks about you as an artist and as a character. A canvas doesn't sell just because it's cheap or technically impeccable. It is sold because it's yours.

5.3 The right attitude

It could be that you are shy, reserved and a person of few words. Regardless of that fact, I recommend that when you are among people, you adopt a sociable and outgoing attitude, this is a rule that applies to any sales job. For an artist it is much more important since in most cases you are the only one who can promptly promote the sale of his work. Try to always be approachable, talk to people, smile and always have a nice demeanor. Whenever it is appropriate, do not hesitate to say that you are an artist. Many people like this, even the ones who are not than interested in art. It will be an excellent opportunity to reach out and invite new guests to your events or workshops. Never miss the opportunity to request contact information that will benefit your database.

Always try to behave in a way that does not generate any kind of negative reaction in others. I'm not saying that everyone has to like you. But pay attention not to adopt unfriendly behaviors because it could affect you in the long run. Try to generate sympathy and a good predisposition with potential clients. When you participate in a special event, consider it a job. Try not to overindulge in alcoholic beverages that could make you act differently in front of others. Take it in moderation, always maintain a good attitude and impeccable behavior.

5.4 What people expect of you

When a potential client wants to purchase one of your pieces, they are usually motivated by two reasons:

- They like the aesthetic of the piece and want to use it for decorative purposes
- They consider it an investment because they think your career will eventually grow and so will your prices.

In some cases, it's a combination of both. People don't usually buy a piece they don't like or they won't resell in the future. How do regular people evaluate you as an artist and get an idea about the future growth of your work? Most people have no idea and maybe neither do you. No one can know how lucky you will be in your career in the coming years, so the only thing they can assess is the aesthetics of your work and your professional image. What are they evaluating in you to convince themselves to buy one of your pieces at the asking price?

First, they look for a discount to have the idea of having paid it for less than what it was worth. This is very easy to demonstrate because you have your work on eBay, art galleries and classifieds. You have advertised at high prices and you are giving them a special discount because they are personally buying a piece from you. Buyers value these types of discounts. They will display it and look proud and will tell everyone the name of the artists who offered them a special discount. He will be honored and will speak highly of you to his friends and family. Some of them might contact you to congratulate you and ask you to please sell them pieces at a discount price. You are realizing at this stage that you are beginning to reap everything you have sowed previously. Buyers in most cases don't know anything about art, and are looking for an artist who is on Wikipedia, who has their own website, who is active on social media, participates in auctions and cultural events, etc.

They are looking for a person with a professional career who gives him the idea of staying very active and present at all events. They want to see someone that works hard to continually grow their career as an artist. Some clients will feel part of a team that has to work with you to increase your fame as an artist and the value of your works. Your clients will speak highly of you and promote your work without asking for anything in return.

If you apply all these strategies with determination and continuity, people will see in you the image of a successful and professional artists whose asking price per piece will eventually go up. Then they will be willing to pay you what you ask for each of them. The world if full of artistic snobs who are unfriendly, poorly dressed and misunderstood. Don't be one of them. They may not understand your art, but they will buy your work if they like the person you are and the image of the artist you created by following all tips included in this book.

5.5 How to keep in touch with clients and followers

It's very important that you keep in constant touch with everyone who appreciates your artwork. Constant interaction with them will allow you to further increase the number of your followers and as a consequence, sales will follow. You will have two types of fans: those in your database and those in your social networks. Each of them requires a different treatment for the interaction to be productive. Those in your database are all the people that you have personally met through networking events. You can reach these people directly due to the fact that you have their contact information.

Keep them updated on what you are working on, what events you are participating in and future art exhibitions. Most of them will be honored and happy to hear from you. I suggest you use their phone numbers with discretion, meaning only use them for direct invitations to an event. It is very important that you write personalized messages to each one, greeting them cordially and by their name and also thanking them in advance for their attention or participation in the event. Try not to send chain messages or SPAM mail unless your list has grown so much that it is almost impossible to send personalized messages. In this case, try to personalize messages only to those who have already bought a piece from you or those you know very well. **Important tip**: never send commercial offers directly to your WhatsApp. It is too invasive and indiscreet. Send you offers by email as it is more discreet and professional. This category of people represents a select group of passionate individuals who know you very well and admire you. Whenever possible, give them something as a thank you for being your fans. Some create ideas for inexpensive gifts are:

- Create a piece only for your fans and send it via email in high resolution. Declare that you will maintain the original in your permanent collection which is unavailable for sale. Recommend your contacts to print it and take it to your next event so you can autograph it,
- Write a short e-book with your biography some interesting stories about your art and send it as a gift to all of your fans
- Organize an art class and only invite your fans. Each person can only invite one more person.

- Send them a digital survey asking them what they want the theme of your next piece to be. It also works well to ask them where they would like you to organize your next event.

Your fans will be happy to interact with you in this way. Remember that after yourself and perhaps a few family members, they are the ones who most admire you.

Obviously, the management of followers on social media networks is very different from that of your direct contacts. I recommend a minimum of three weekly posts and a maximum of one daily post on both Facebook and Instagram. A photo, video or a story about your work. You decide how to communicate on each social network. Remember that it is important to use high quality material, cultural content, excellent resolution, etc. For YouTube, I recommend that you post video courses on your techniques, work in progress videos, coverage of art exhibits, interviews and any other high-quality cultural material that is related to your artist profile. Don't improvise anything because it looks unprofessional. Remember that everything you do has to be consistent and in resonance with your artistic profile. It is better that your content related to your work be serious, professional and culturally interesting. If not, you better not post anything because it would be counterproductive. An important detail is that you do not fill your social networks with you works of art. Also publish content from other colleagues and details of your life outside of art. A profile only focused on your creations looks more like a product catalog than an interesting source of content.

5.6 How to handle criticism

The correct way to handle criticism is a very delicate and complex subject. Knowing how to handle it correctly is very important for anyone, whatever their job may be. To not stray away from the main subject of this book, lets cover criticism received in the workplace. Usually, any employee, businessman or salesman receives criticism from clients, colleagues, superiors or subordinates. Normally its related to work and anything going on in the work environment. For an artist it's not always like this. The fact that you can showcase your work on several platforms, both on and off, exposes you to criticism from people who are not your clients. People will comment on your work without being interested and even worse, they might not know much about art. Unfortunately, this type of criticism is common and you will have to be very prepared to react in the best way possible. You must realize that normally criticism is not directed at you as a person or as a human being. Most of it will be directed towards your work. It's normal that there will be people who do not appreciate your creations.

Even if you were the best artists in the world in your fields, odds are not everyone is going to like you, but in the end, this is not necessary. The important thing is that your work is liked by a select group of fans that you stay in contact with. Let's put it this way, you are not a politician that needs a minimum number of voters or he won't be chosen. Not even Gandhi or Pope John Paul II had the total support of their people. A lot of people hated them. They received physical assault, insults, bullets and still they were very successful.

They were never defeated or intimidated by haters. Another interesting point is that you can use criticism as a resource to grow as a human being and as a salesperson. If we do not pay attention to insults directed towards you as a person or your family, the rest are for your art work and this can sometimes help you. When you receive criticism about your prices, do not tell the person that its maybe because they don't have the resources to buy it. This is probably true, but respond kindly. You can probably say that you will try to produce smaller pieces in the future so they can be affordable if and when it still allows you to properly express your art form. When you receive criticism about very large sized pieces, answer the same way and take the opportunity to really assess whether it is worth producing works of smaller sizes.

Perhaps you will increase your sales and it is thanks to these reviews. When you receive comments about topics related to your art such as colors, shapes, subjects simply tell them that at this stage of your life as an artist, this is what you feel and how you have managed to express it. Perhaps in another stage, you have different inspirations that lead you to produce different things. When you receive criticism about an event or exhibition that you have organized, listen carefully because in this case you could benefit and improve certain details that you might have overlooked. Always thank people who take the trouble to comment on your work.

Good or bad, the comment is an opportunity for you to improve. Never forget it. So far, we have covered face-to-face criticism. The same is true for the criticism and comments you receive on social networks. Respond kindly and always thank everyone. Use these comments to improve and not to discourage you. Also, when receiving harsh opinions from art critics or experts, I recommend you don't ignore them. They are valuable and they will probably help you improve your sales. Remember that you decide whether to receive criticism as a blow to the face or as a valuable resource. It all depends on how you react.

5.7 Your work in objects, accessories, gadgets. Pros and Cons

There are ways to monetize your artistic talent by selling accessories. There are many gadgets that you can personalize with your art, but handle this subject with care because it does not lend itself to valuing all artists. I will only mention a few and it is up to you to assess whether its suitable for your profile or not. Each one has pros and cons, depending on the type of artist you are and the nature of your work. Choosing the appropriate form is extremely important and it is the only thing that makes sense of a business strategy.

To be honest, I have not always liked what I have seen and that is why I wanted to write about this. You have to choose only one product that has a culturally compatible meaning with your art. I will explain what I mean well and then get some practical examples. Your purpose as an artist is to see works of art and make a living. Whatever you do is fine as long as it's something that gives visibility to your work, to yourself as an artist and could perhaps drive your sales.

You want to value yourself as an artist and earn money. There are things you can do and things that are not advisable. Only you can choose what's right for you. If you're a painter or a sculptor, what in my opinion improves your image and gives you more visibility and prestige is to put your work on the label of a good wine, the cover of a book, in the manifesto of a theatrical work, etc. They are things that improve and increase your artistic cultural value. What does not benefit your artist profile is to print your work on mugs, plates, T-Shirts, shoes, key chains and bags & accessories. I do not recommend doing this because you would give the idea of not being successful with the sales of your work and that you're looking for other ways to get ahead in your career. There is nothing wrong with looking for other sources of income, but do it with your artwork. Even if you are successful and earn some money, this strategy would be like rowing against your career as an artist. If you want to get into this business you can do it, but do not use your paintings or signature.

Use completely new material. Design things separately for each project. Things that give you a new identity as a designer of shirts or bags, for example. In this way you create an artist independent on your professional image. They are two very different things and it is not always convenient to mix them. I have met several talented painters who exhibit in contemporary art museums and at the same time sell hand painted caps.

I have also seen some who paint shoes, shirts, plastic bottles for gyms, etc. I see nothing wrong with customizing these accessories but this is no longer the work of an artists, it is the work of a craftsman. I do not want to be misinterpreted for what I just mentioned.

There is nothing wrong with working as an artisan, but if you do it by reproducing and copying your work you will give the impression of being an artist who is not successful. I doubt that you will do much to carry out this type of artisan work. Usually the emotion is so much at first, but it fades when you realize all the time it costs you to make these products and then sell them very cheap. These objects do not have the same profit margin that your art offers you in its traditional form. If you want to also work as an artisan, you can do it simultaneously with your artist career. But do it with a different profile and a brand of the artist you already are.

Create another style, something that has its own identity and that is not identified with your other works. Sign with a different stage name. This can go a long way if you find the right formula, but do not do anything that can work against all the work you do to grow as a traditional artist.

CHAPTER 6

MOTIVATIONAL TIPS

6.1 Search for inspiration

We have almost reached the end of your learning process. Now you know what you can do to maximize sales and thus come to live only off of the fruits of your art. This is every artist's dream. If you lack ideas or inspiration, I recommend you read and travel as much as possible, visit art exhibitions and do everything that makes you feel good.

The fact that you are working hard and are determined will guide you to the path of inspiration. If you lack the financial resources to get ahead, start little by little and work on something else in the meantime, but don't give up on your dream, because only you can make it come true. You will receive support but nobody can ever do it for you.

6.2 Search for life coaches that help you grow

Did you know that all successful professionals have one or more coaches? I don't mean people who work exclusively for you, it would be too expensive and only few can afford such an expense. I'm talking about looking for people to help you improve aspects of your profession in which you are weaker and less prepared.

We are all very good at some things and less good at others and to optimize the performance of our businesses, we have to consult professionals just in the areas where we are scarce. You can have a coach to help you analyze work production strategies, save on materials, optimize production times and choose the topics that are the most fashionable on the market.

Also, another that is in charge of designing a sales strategy tailored to your professional profile. Artists and their work are not all the same and need small adjustments to always be effective. It would also be nice to have someone to advise you on your personal image. There are many fields in which professional help may be needed to improve out income. Your purpose is to live from your art and for this reason you will need a bit of help that will make your life easier and make your professional efforts more effective. There are good coaches who will provide you their services remotely and will cost you very little, compared to the benefits that their consultations will bring you. Do not hesitate to contact and use them.

6.3 Sell your work for the benefits they bring and not for the characteristics they have

Regardless of the characteristics of a product in any commercial transaction, the buyer decides when they like the benefits that will obtain with what he or she purchases. The same thing happens with art. When you are negotiating with a potential client, don't just talk about the technical characteristics of a piece such as materials and measurements. This is not going to convince them to buy it.

To sell you have to highlight the benefits that you will get with your work. You can tell them that it will make their office look more colorful, their living room more luminous and/or their apartment more elegant. You will also tell them that based on your commercial strategies, the prices of your work will increase a lot in the next 5 years. This is what everyone wants to hear. Depending on the type of art you sell, you should always focus on the benefits.

6.4 Other Tips

Advice for art teachers

If you are an art teacher, I hope you liked this book to the point of recommending it to your students. I know this may come out of your subject or professional responsibility towards them, but it is something that will undoubtedly be useful to you as soon as you finish your studies and leave school. Do not let any of them be forced to repress their talent and give up their career as an artist for not being able to market their work. It would be a pleasure and an honor for me to contribute to the human and professional growth of your students. They are people who have studied art because they love it. The vast majority of them want to live from art. They will be much more comfortable and successful if someone teaches them how to sell their work. A talented artist is fulfilled and successful if he knows how to sell his work at the best price.

Advice for art students

If you are an art student who is about to leave the academy and enter the world of artists, never give up on the dream of living from your work. At first it may be hard, but little by little you will succeed. You have to be strong and determined to get what you want.

Do not be discouraged, not even in the most difficult moments. You have talent and you know it, you just have to find inspiration to produce work and discipline to be able to sell them. If you learn to sell your artwork, your life will be easier.

Advice for parents of aspiring artists

If your child wants to dedicate their life to art, I imagine you might be concerned about their future. Good parents always care about the financial stability of their children. Also, the idea of them having to pay for their expenses and support their future families with income from their artwork probably makes you nervous. It is completely understandable and normal to feel this way. If you allow me to give you some advice, don't try to oppose their path or come between their desire to do this for a living. If you can, try to help them learn how to sell. Artists are very special people because they belong in the category of people who love their work.

There are not many special people like them in the world. Most people reluctantly work 8 hours a day, long for the weekends and do what they like only in their spare time. The artist does what he or she likes everyday even if it means to have poor economic stability. Art is their passion, do not come between a person and their passion. Support them as much as you can because the world needs more people like them. There are several ways to help a child as he or she tries to find their way in the art world. Some are very obvious, such as supporting them financially so they can study, get tools and any other material aid as they make their way to becoming an artist. There is another way to show support: your emotional support as a parent.

No one needs more emotional support from their relatives than an artist. Make them feel that you support them and blindly believe in their talent. Help him extend invitations to friends and family to participate in his exhibits and try to give them any help you can. I repeat, no one but an artist needs more moral support from their parents. If you are concerned about his financial future, the only thing you could do is try to convince him to look for a part time job to help them through their journey of becoming an artist. This allows them to have a little more economic stability and financial freedom. Help them find balance in their lives but do not oppose their passion for art. Things have changed a lot in the work environment.

It is easier today to earn money as an artist thanks to all the tools and media available. On the other hand, earning a living with a traditional professional career is no longer as easy as before. Today, multinational banks, insurance companies and even entire countries go bankrupt. Times have changed and so has the economy. You also need to change the way you think about money and the work environment.

Advice for family and friends of an artist

If you are reading this book and you are not an artist, you may have a friend or family member who is. Of course, they need a bit of your help. With this I am not saying that you need to buy one of their pieces. You are probably not interested in art or you don't like his or her work. You might also not have the budget to invest in this but surely there are other ways you can show your support. For example, when there is an art exhibition, participate and invite all of your friends. You'll have a glass of wine, meet new people and bask in the art culture. You can post invitations to events on your social networks. It does not cost you anything and it would be very helpful. Art is fabulous and it's always good to support these initiatives. Everyone wins.

Advice for influencers and vendors who negotiate with an artist

If you are an influencer who knows how to monetize their social networks, you will probably sometimes come across artists who ask you to promote their work with posts and stories. I'm not asking you to give your work away, but you can offer a discount or help out in any way. It would be great. Artists always have few resources to promote their art and events. Most of them earn very little and continue to work in art out of pure love and feeling. If you support them, you will be doing it for a noble cause. Always treat them in a special way.

Consider that your service does not have labor or raw material costs, it is only a post and you have the margin to offer a generous discount. If you are a vendor or supplier, you'll probably have lower margins compared to influencers. Whenever possible, I encourage you to support the artists as much as you can. We all owe something to art. If we consider all the times we have enjoyed a painting, statue or any other form of art, most of the times they were free experiences. We have a debt and must support art whenever possible.

Create your brand and mark as an artist

People have to recognize your artistic style from a distance. If they see a work of art created by you, they should recognize it without seeing your signature. If you succeed, you will have achieved your mark as an artist. This tip has nothing to do with sales strategies, I often meet artists who need it. The first objective you have to achieve after leaving art school is to personalize your style and characterize your work. It is not only necessary to sign a piece with your name and excite the observer with your techniques and talent.

Your work must speak for itself. Your work must be immediately associated with yourself. When you see a work of art by Van Gogh from afar, be it authentic or a replica, you immediately identify it. This is essential for art collectors to fall in love with you as an artist and always recognize you. You are an artist and you know what I mean. Work hard to identify your mark as an artist.

Become a businessperson and your work's best salesperson

If you want to make a living from this you have to learn how to sell. You must become an entrepreneur and the best salesperson of your own work. You are the one who thinks, performs and owns the work. No one can sell it better than you will succeed as long as you have discipline applying the appropriate sales strategies.

Your art is not for everyone

Do not make the mistake of thinking that your art is for everyone because it is not like that. It would be something very difficult to achieve and I do not see any logical or commercial sense. Your art should be for a specific niche, a select group of people who feel emotion when they admire your work. If you try to please everyone, you become a custom craftsman. There is nothing wrong with this, but you would not be an artist. Create a community of people who identify with your artistic seal and interact with them frequently.

CHAPTER 7

HOW TO CREATE 104,000 DOLLARS IN WORKS OF ART

I decided to create a separate chapter to talk about this as it is very important. In the art world, the value of a work does not only depend on the materials that were used to create it. It depends on who made it. The author's signature generally determines the price range much more than the materials used.

A work of art by an unknown artist who does not promote his work is worth little more than the materials invested in its creation. This type of artist is called ARTISAN. On the contrary, a very famous artists can sell work at a much higher price. Also, when using the same materials as a craftsman.

The time of the famous artist is worth more than the time of a stranger. Between these two extreme cases, there is plenty of space where you can position yourself as a professional. It is about applying strategies that help you sell your work at more expensive prices. The better known you are, the more your work is worth. That is why you cannot dedicate your life only to producing them. You have to know how to sell them.

No matter how good they are, nobody will buy them if your sales strategies are not good and your marketing is scarce. You need people to know and recognize your brand as an artist. However, I am going to explain how it is relatively simple to create an inventory that is worth 104.000. It seems like a very high and ambitious number, but it is doable. To simplify the explanation. I will make the example of a painter although any artist can apply it, changing the parameters in due time on their art.

It starts with producing the following work:

20 very small paintings at 400 USD each = 8,000 USD

20 small paintings at 600 USD each = 12,000 USD

10 medium paintings at 800 USD each = 8,000 USD

10 large paintings at 1,500 USD each = 15,000 USD

10 larger paintings at 3,000 USD each =15,000 USD

1 gigantic piece at 6,000 USD = 6,000 USD

200 lithographs or impressions at 200 USD each = 40,000 USD

This adds up to an inventory of 104,000 USD to sell. Of course, you will have to invest at least 5,000 USD for materials and many hours of work. Obviously, you are not obliged to create all of these works of art at once. You will be able to vary characteristics, prices and quantities according to the availability of time and money that you have.

I made this example in order to help you see that there are quite simple ways to work some materials and put them up for sale at a value of 104,000 USD. It is not done overnight but you have to know that it is feasible. I also did it to explain in a simple way that what you do is not worth much if you consider only the materials and the time you invest. Your work will be worth these prices only if you promote your artist career with a suitable commercial strategy. Otherwise, no one will buy your work at the prices I have indicated. Prices that will allow you to live comfortably from your art. Good artists do it and you can too. Go ahead!

CHAPTER 8

ARTIST SUCCESS STORIES

There are many stories of famous artists who during their lives had to face enormous problems and difficulties. Their invaluable talent could not have found a way to manifest themselves if each of them had not been tenacious, determined and unwavering. Their talent was as great as their confidence in their art. No one could see it this way, except themselves. This was the only thing that allowed their talent to flourish and be imprinted in the history of art forever. I put these motivational stories at the end of the book because I didn't want to interrupt your learning process.

I wanted you to read everything in the shortest possible time without being distracted by other topics. I decided to write these stories at the end, when all the commercial issues about sales have already been dealt with. These stories are very motivating and you can read them when you need a little help to regain some inspiration and enthusiasm. Enjoy and be inspired by them as they are a great source of motivation that you will constantly need throughout your career as an artist.

Saving Mr. Banks

It is a beautiful film that talks about the life of Walt Disney, which despite enormous fame and undoubted success in his business, had many obstacles early in his career. He was rejected several times because his drawings didn't seem interesting and was accused of not being very creative. Yes, I am talking about Walt Disney. Guess what it was that drove him to success: the determination and perseverance of working hard, always trusting himself without losing motivation every time he went bankrupt. This was what helped him get ahead so that his talent did the rest. Do not forget, you have to believe in yourself, always try one more time and NEVER give up. This is the only difference between successful talented people and unsuccessful talented people.

Vincent Van Gogh

We all know his name and have seen some of his work at some point. I was fortunate and honored to visit his museum in the city of Amsterdam in 2000 and was impressed by his work. I still remember the emotions I felt when standing in front of each of his paintings. I still do not understand how no one could get so excited during van Gogh's lifetime. No one expressed the interest he deserved. In fact, the painter was recognized as a great artist only a few years after his death.

What would motivate you about his life? Surely not his poverty or his mental problems. What I find very motivating is his determination to continue painting and evolving his style, despite the fact that nobody was very interested in his work. How many talented artists like Van Gogh decided to give up and change jobs? How many beautiful works of art were never created just for lack of determination and perseverance? I always ask myself these questions every time I think of artists who followed their passions and love for art despite economic hardships in their lives.

I also think that many of them if they had lived in this era could have had powerful tools that perhaps would have helped them become successful during their lifetime. You have these tools at your disposal and at very cheap prices. You may not be equipped with even a tenth of Van Gogh's artistic talent but you can prepare to make a living from art and earn a lot of money selling your work. You can live a very comfortable life and earn much more than him.

Never forget these advantages that many artists that came before you did not have.

In the Pursuit of Happyness

I'll be honest, I have seen this movie at least 20 times and although it has nothing to do with art, I highly recommend it. It is beautiful and will help motivate you whenever you need it. Its leading actor, Will Smith, plays Chris Gardner, an American businessman who in the 1980's had to face serious financial problems and a complicated divorce. He lived a year in extreme poverty, sleeping on the street while caring for his son Christopher without anyone's help. You probably won't have to go through these hardships to excel as an artist and your rise to success is sure to be less dramatic. I suggest to watch the film carefully and focus on the determination to rise with which the protagonist faces the difficulties in his life. Look also at the advice he gives his son. think of Chris's biography and movie every time you think you can't so something or anytime you want to give up in business. I am very grateful to everyone who contributed to the creation of this film. For me it is a work of art and an infinite source of motivation and good energy. The talent of the producer and all of the actors is immensely great. THANK YOU!

CONCLUSION

You have reached the end of this book. I wrote it inspired by my enormous love for art. A passion that only grows through time. I could not be an artist since I have no particular talent for it. What motivated me while I was writing this was the desire to help others push their talents. I want to do it globally so that everyone can learn to live from their art. Teaching you a step by step how to sell their work through a book is the fastest and cheapest way I found how to do it. I have tried to be as accurate as possible so that the reader can learn only the necessary information.

It is in my nature to reach a goal in the shortest time possible, at least with expenses and resources. Time is the most valuable resource we have and I did not want to waste yours more than necessary. It is an immense pleasure and great honor to be able to contribute to accomplishing your dreams to having a successful life as an artist with financial stability. It is very important to know that I can support your professional growth.

In the back of my mind, I also dream about art but in a different way than an artist might.

THANK YOU for reading this book, I hope you enjoyed it.

THANK YOU for being an artist and for sharing your emotions with people who admire your work.

THANK YOU for trusting me. I wish you good luck and a lot of success in your journey as an artist.

www.ingramcontent.com/pod-product-compliance
Ingram Content Group UK Ltd.
Pitfield, Milton Keynes, MK11 3LW, UK
UKHW040032200726
13854UKWH00001B/481